Fighting for Survival
The Dani of Irian Jaya

Liz Thompson

Reed Library
Cardigan Street

Dedication and acknowledgements

This book is dedicated to the Dani people.

I would like to thank Simon Coate for his support and assistance during the journey to Irian Jaya. I would also like to thank Jim Elmslie, Mark Worth, Mark Davies and Ben Bohane for their help with additional information and quotations.

Acknowledgement and thanks also go to Leica Cameras, Vision Graphics Photographic and Imaging Services, Jungle Boys Studios and Fujifilm Australia, without whose support this book would not have been possible.

First published 1997 by
Reed Library•Cardigan Street
an imprint of Reed Reference Australia, part of Reed Educational &
Professional Publishing, 18–22 Salmon Street, Port Melbourne,
Victoria 3207, Australia (a division of Reed International Books
Australia Pty Ltd, ACN 001-002-357).

Ⓡ A Reed Elsevier company

Edited by Wendy Skilbeck
Designed by Jo Waite Design
Typeset in Optima 11/14pt
Production by Cindy Smith
Printed in Hong Kong by H & Y Printing Ltd

Cover photograph: A Dani elder in traditional dress of necklace of bark and cowrie shells, wearing pig tusks through his nose and with hair braided and mixed with pig fat.

National Library of Australia
Cataloguing-in-publication data:

Thompson, Liz, 1963-.
The Dani of Irian Jaya.

Bibliography.
Includes Index.

ISBN 1 86391 032 8.

1. Dani (New Guinea people) - Foreign influences - Juvenile literature. 2. Dani (New Guinea people) - Social life and customs - Juvenile literature. I. Title. (Series: Fighting for survival).

306.089995

Contents

Early morning at Wamena markets.

Introduction

Diary

Sunday, October 1st (1995)

Flying across the border from Papua New Guinea I am struck by the endless rainforest that stretches across the mountains. Shortly after crossing the border the plane approaches Jayapura, the capital of Irian Jaya. The long, straight roads, which symbolise the face of Indonesian rule, cut across the landscape. Rows of small, square houses sit like soldiers on either side of the roads. The difference between this and the meandering pathways of Papua New Guinea, where the towns and villages stretch across the ground with a random pattern that shows a disregard for order, is striking. These formations are a sign of the differences that divide Papua New Guinea and Irian Jaya. These differences are made stranger by the fact that the people of both countries are Melanesians with similar cultures and customs. Prior to the division of the island by colonial authorities, Papua New Guinea and Irian Jaya were one land inhabited by one people, Melanesians.

Colonial history

West New Guinea, as Irian Jaya was previously known, formed part of the Dutch East Indies colonial empire. When the Dutch signed an agreement with the Sultan of Tidore in 1660, it fell under Dutch control. During the Second World War, West New Guinea was invaded by the Japanese. The Dutch regained control after the war ended but Indonesia now claimed independence. From 1945 to 1949 the Indonesians were at war with the Dutch and over 100,000 Indonesians were killed. Finally, in 1949, the Dutch East Indies was granted independence. This area became the state of Indonesia but it did not include West New Guinea, which remained with the Dutch.

A Dani woman who lives in the Baliem Valley in the heart of Irian Jaya. The Dani, like the rest of the Irianese, are Melanesians, culturally quite different to the Indonesians who govern them.

Moves towards independence

The Dutch started to assist West New Guinea on the path to becoming an independent Melanesian state. They developed communications and transportation facilities and encouraged an expectation of independence among the local people.

Indonesia's aspirations

At the same time Indonesia, under the leadership of President Sukarno, commenced an enormous campaign in an effort to gain control of West New Guinea. The USA supported the Indonesian view, hoping to gain influence over Indonesia, fearing that it might fall under the influence of the USSR and communism. In the face of this kind of support the Dutch gave up their hopes for West New Guinean independence and signed the New York Agreement in 1962. West New Guinea became known as 'Irian Barat' and fell under the control of the United Nations.

'Vote of Free Choice' or 'Vote Free of Choice'

The United Nations approved the Indonesian takeover of Irian Jaya but they imposed a condition. The agreement was that within five years there would be a 'Vote of Free Choice' among the Irianese as to whether or not they wished to maintain Indonesian rule. At the time of the event the Indonesian military rounded up 1025 Irianese leaders and forced them to vote. The outcome was obviously in favour of Indonesian rule and became known as the 'Vote Free of Choice'. West New Guinea was called Irian Jaya, which means 'Victorious Irian', and officially became a part of Indonesia. In Biak, a local language, 'Iryan' meant something quite different: 'a steamy land rising from the sea'.

'They are different to us; our hair, our land, our skin is different, we are black, our tradition and customs, many things are different.'
Kelly Kwalik, leader of the central command of the Organisasi Papua Merdeka (OPM), or Free Papua Movement, in an interview with Ben Bohane

The Indonesian regime

Diary
Wednesday, October 4th (1995)

Landing at the airport in Irian Jaya, the plane is met by Indonesian officials. The air is thick with the sweet smell of clove cigarettes so popular among Indonesians. The airport has expanded since my last visit four years ago. An hour of driving along winding coastal roads at break-neck speed brings me to Jayapura.

Everywhere is activity. Where you expect Melanesians there are Indonesian street vendors frying bean curd and brewing thick, sweet coffee. Buildings and shanties line the edge of the river. Pop music and traffic noise fills the streets. Falling silent in the afternoon heat, the town takes a siesta. In the cooler hours of evening, oil lamps swing from the beams of market stalls. Only a handful of Irianese wandering in from the outlying villages and a local market full of indigenous carvings reminds me that I am in fact in Irian Jaya, a Melanesian country, and not in the heart of Asia.

A framed picture of President Suharto, the Indonesian president, at the doorway of a poster shop.

Since taking over Irian Jaya, Indonesia has done its utmost to Indonesianise the Irianese; that is, to make the Melanesian Irianese as Indonesian as possible. The two groups have very different religious and cultural traditions. They have different ideas about many things such as land ownership, freedom and the rights of individuals to express themselves. Attempts to Indonesianise the Irianese have met with resistance, and many thousands of Irianese have died since the Indonesian takeover. It is not permitted to speak out publicly against the regime and disobedience is dealt with through harsh punishment and lengthy prison sentences. In 1989 a man was imprisoned for twenty years for flying the West Papuan flag, The Morning Star, and his wife was sentenced to eight years for sewing it.

'The Morning Star is derived from an ancient Papuan legend where the morning star (Venus) took on a human form and came to represent the force of good. As Venus heralds the coming dawn, so flying the flag will hasten the coming of freedom.'
**Robin Osborne, 'The Flag That Won't Go Away',
Inside Indonesia, no. 4, March 1985, p. 29**

A Dani man from the Baliem Valley, in which there were local uprisings in 1977 and 1984, wears a discarded Indonesian military uniform.

Military

Throughout Indonesia there is a strong military presence in the effort to maintain order. This is particularly so in Irian Jaya. Everywhere you see soldiers in uniform walking casually in the streets. In Wamena and the Baliem Valley, the area this book explores, the military presence is even greater after uprisings in 1977 and 1984 and many years of unrest.

Organisasi Papua Merdeka (OPM)

In response to the strict rule experienced under the Indonesian regime and the growing desire among many Irianese for independence, the Organisasi Papua Merdeka (OPM), or Free Papua Movement, was established. The OPM is a freedom fighting movement that is committed to achieving independence for Irian Jaya. No one is sure how many people belong to the organisation: estimates range between 200 and 50,000. Statistics show that around 40,000 men between the ages of 19 and 29 years are unaccounted for and it is quite possible that many of these men are with the OPM, who live and fight in the jungles of Irian Jaya.

Suparjo, the ever-present face of the Indonesian military.

Struggle

There have been a number of uprisings in various parts of the country. In his unpublished thesis, Jim Elmslie says that these uprisings have met with a rapid and harsh military response from the Indonesian Armed Forces who use helicopter gunships, jets dropping napalm, and executions as well as actual combat. The highest death toll has been cited by the Anti-Slavery Society in London. It believes as many as 300,000 Irianese have been killed.

Resource exploitation

Various foreign companies have established mines in Irian Jaya. The biggest and best known is the copper mine P. T. Freeport Indonesia, whose largest shareholder is Macmaran Copper and Gold USA. Freeport has the largest published gold reserves in the world. Tailings that flow out from the mine are polluting local river systems and the Amungme people who traditionally own the land have received practically no compensation or share of the profits. **(Photograph courtesy of Jim Elmslie)**

Alongside their efforts to culturally absorb the Irianese, the Indonesians have taken advantage of the enormous potential for resource exploitation. Like Papua New Guinea there is abundant gold and copper to be mined as well as some of the world's largest areas of virgin rainforest to be logged, and many mineral reserves. In most cases the local people have received inadequate, if any, compensation for the cutting of their forests or the mining of their land.

'We are angry with Freeport because the company came here and is exploiting everything. We have a tradition, a custom. If someone comes to our garden and takes a pig or birds or fruit and they don't tell us, we can kill them, because that is our traditional law. Freeport came here and took everything from this land, the minerals, gold and trees, only for themselves and the Indonesian Government, and never gave us any compensation. Every day there is pollution in the water and many fish and plants are killed. People drink the water and they get sick and their body is not good. We don't agree with this and we are angry with Freeport.'

Kelly Kwalik, leader of the central command of the OPM, in an interview with Ben Bohane

The young face of an Indonesian transmigrant in Irian Jaya.

Transmigration

Irian Jaya makes up approximately 20 per cent of the land mass of the whole of Indonesia and it is a relatively unpopulated country. Many parts of Indonesia are chronically overcrowded and the Indonesian Government set up a series of transmigration programs through which large numbers of Indonesians were moved to Irian Jaya. They were given some financial assistance and a plot of land. This meant that, despite the fact that land ownership is at the heart of Melanesian culture, land was taken from the Irianese with little or no compensation being paid. The Indonesians considered all non-cultivated land belonged to the state, and argued that the development that they brought to Irian Jaya was more than adequate compensation for the loss of land. Today 25 per cent of the population of Irian Jaya are Indonesians and the numbers are expected to continue rising.

Diary
Wednesday, October 4th (1995)

After finding a small hotel I try to work out what time the planes leave each day for Wamena in the Baliem Valley. During the wet season flights are cancelled frequently when a thick blanket of cloud descends and the planes cannot land.

It is the Baliem Valley in which the Dani tribe live. One of the most beautiful places I have ever seen. Last time I was here signs of change were obvious. I know that a great deal will be different now.

The land of the Dani

Diary
Friday, October 6th (1995)

Flying into the Baliem Valley the scenery is breathtakingly beautiful. Mountain tops reach towards the heavens and around them thin wisps of cloud spiral. Below broad, winding rivers and waterfalls cut through the valleys. Extraordinary terracing systems etch patterns into the mountainsides. The Dani, renowned for their sophisticated gardening systems, grow crops on slopes so sheer that women have to tend them suspended on vine ropes.

As we landed in Wamena, I looked out of the window. On my previous visits I felt I had travelled a thousand years back in time. Beyond the wire fence surrounding the airport were perhaps a hundred Irianese. The women wore skirts made of rolled bark and orchid vine; the men wore penis gourds and were decorated with feathers, dried yellow daisies and long neckties made of tiny white cowrie shells. They carried bows and arrows and pigs under their arms. Outside the airport a Dani, naked but for a gourd, his hair rolled into tiny strands and smothered in pig fat, looked at himself in the rear view mirror of a 250cc Yamaha motorbike. As I left the airport people stood and watched in fascination.

Shrouded in the mystical quality of early morning mist, villagers brought their produce to Wamena markets. They carried bilum bags filled with green vegetables and sweet potato, they smoked tobacco rolled up in dry leaves and organised vegetables in coloured pyramids. Everything was of earth hues. Amidst this picture appeared signs of change. One Dani wore a plastic Wella showercap on his braided hair. Nylon string replaced the rolled bark used to make bilum bags and naked men and women jumped from the paths of small cars and scooters. The encroachment of the twentieth century was painfully evident.

Today as I peered from the window, almost all the Irianese watching the plane land wore clothes and a large extension was being built onto the departures and arrivals lounge. As I left the airport I was followed by Dani with plastic bags from which they pulled gourds and woven bracelets for sale. They followed me down the street trying to take me to certain hotels. My heart sank as I realised how much change had taken place in such a short period of time.

Dani outside an Indonesian restaurant in Wamena. All restaurants and hotels in Wamena are owned by Indonesians.

Wamena

Wamena used to be a sleepy little administrative capital in the district of Jayawijaya. Today it is the largest town serviced by air in the world. As yet there is no road joining Wamena with other parts of Irian Jaya. All food and supplies arrive on the daily flights, which means that things are very expensive. All this will soon change. The Trans-Irian Highway, which will connect Jayapura on the south coast with Merauke on the north coast will pass through Wamena. When this road is opened, the huge influx of people and new influences that will come with it will have a dramatic impact on the local community.

Billboards advertise sexually explicit Indonesian films — a new experience for the Dani.

The Baliem Valley

'The only place in the world where man has improved on nature . . . as close to Paradise as one can get.'

'The land of these Dani is the Grand Valley of the Baliem River, a broad, temperate plain lying five thousand feet [1525 metres] above the tropical jungles of New Guinea. At least fifty thousand Dani live in the densely settled valley floor, and another fifty thousand inhabit the scattered settlements along the steep-sided valleys around the Grand Valley. Temperature is mild, rainfall moderate, wildlife harmless and disease rare; this is surely one of the most pleasant corners of man's world.'
R. Gardner and K. G. Heider, **Gardens of War, *p. 8***

A waterfall in the Baliem Valley.

The Baliem River and the winding paths shrouded by trees that run along its edge are found amidst jagged quartzite rocks that rupture the highest grasslands. Everywhere is green, air is clean, water flows fresh and cold from mountain streams. Here for possibly 25,000 years the Dani have lived their lives as warriors and farmers. Spontaneous and uninhibited, the Dani grind their teeth in a show of contentment and weep with friends met after long absences.

Young Dani girls at play.

Diary
Thursday, May 11th (1989)

On my first visit to Irian Jaya I spent two days in Wamena and then walked with an interpreter and guide to Miagima village in the Western Baliem. On the way I passed two women who wandered, their tiny bodies literally buried beneath sacks, which they had split up the sides and wore on their heads like capes. After a day's work in the gardens, they walked home quickly along winding pathways and precarious swinging vine bridges, bending occasionally to pick wild strawberries. I stand two feet [61 centimetres] higher than them, twice their size and white. They peer up at me mischievously from beneath these capes breaking into smiles, their eyes crinkling, their hands held across their mouths to hide their laughter. They reach out to touch me and stroke my arms, all the time laughing and eyes shining. 'Lauk Lauk' (hello, hello) they say in Dani and turn and continue on their way. Huge sacks on spindly legs move into the distance and disappear through the hole in the wall that surrounds their village hamlet.

A vine bridge crossing.

Social organisation

Miagima village. The long house is for cooking and two smaller round huts are where the Dani sleep.

Hamlets

The Dani live in village hamlets that are scattered throughout the valley. They call these hamlets a 'sili' and the men in each 'sili' are often related.

Houses are round in shape and look a bit like mushrooms. Each hamlet usually has four or five of these dome-shaped huts and one long house that is divided into two — half is used as a kitchen and half as a home for the pigs. The largest hut is the men's house and in the smaller ones women sleep with the children, joined by their husbands when they are not in the men's house. The hamlet is surrounded by a retaining wall, which has a small arched entrance designed to keep the pigs from straying.

Built of hardwood, the huts are divided into two floors with heavily thatched grass roofs so they look almost like furry animals in the landscape. In the centre of the lower floor is a continually smouldering fire. In the early morning as the mist is rising, smoke filters through the thatch smothering the roof in a thick, white hovering blanket. Men take most of the responsibility for building and it is always a communal activity.

Many hours are spent in the huts, probably more now that warfare is no longer practised. Time is spent talking, cooking and playing small bamboo harps, which the Dani often store in the large holes in their ear lobes.

Diary

Monday, May 15th (1989)

I distinctly remember arriving at one of the villages I was going to stay in during my six-day walk in the Western Baliem. The chief whooped, leapt up and disappeared inside the doorway of his hut on top of which a garden grew, tall green stems and tiny purple flowers growing thick from the thatch. I followed him inside and saw a small central fire over which hung a pot inside which his dinner cooked. He continued to laugh to himself, cracking small, dry sticks and feeding the fire, poking at the embers and crying out with a high voice, sounds of pleasure.

I lay on the straw floor and the ceiling was coated with years of black soot from the endless fire. Someone brought in a small guitar and plucked out notes as his voice, pitched high, sang a strange, haunting melody. Smoke filled the interior of the hut and all I could see were shining eyes and teeth as people laughed and sang and talked. Some of the old men were so bent and wizened they looked like they had been folded into little parcels, like tiny concertinas.

Men's and women's roles

Roles are strictly divided among the Dani, and male and female activities are generally quite separate. Chiefs are always male and men hold much of the power in the community. They often have more than one wife, who they purchase using traditional wealth. Women prepare all the food and take most of the responsibility for bringing up the children.

Shaving facial and pubic hair is another great pastime. Using a piece of bamboo, snapped to form a giant pair of tweezers, they shave one another by pulling out two or three hairs at a time.

Ritualised warfare

Warriors often wore feathers and shell decorations to battle, and sometimes pig tusks through their noses.

'The risks involved in fighting an occasional battle are not nearly as great as those to be encountered were they to ignore the demands of unavenged ghosts.'
R. Gardener and K. G. Heider, Gardens of War, p. 136

Avenging the ancestors

Much of the Dani's time was traditionally spent in the practice of ritualised warfare. Children played war games using small seed warriors and tiny bows and arrows, and learnt of tactical skills from a very young age. Motivation for battles among grown men was usually a desire to pacify the ghosts of dead ancestors. It was believed that if these ancestors had been killed in war their deaths must be avenged or else they became angry with the living. The fear of these ghosts was considerable.

Battles

Battles were fought among various alliances, of which there are a dozen or more in the Baliem Valley. Each alliance spread across an area of about 35 square miles (56 square kilometres). Frontiers were established between each area. These were guarded by tall bamboo and vine watchtowers, which looked ominously towards the horizon. These were almost constantly manned by warriors whose only weapons were bows and arrows. The men would converge on the battlefield as the sun rose, their bodies decorated with white lime, feathers and shells. Battle would commence when both sides were ready. During a day's fighting there would be about ten or twenty clashes. As the sun went down, fighting ceased and the men would return to their own side of the battleground and begin hurling abuse at one another. In the book *Gardens of War,* Robert Gardner describes the insults as personal and often leading to a great deal of laughter from both camps. Late in the evening people from far-lying villages would begin to make their way home.

Casualties

Casualties were very few. According to first-hand accounts, the Dani were more concerned with practising tactics and competence in dodging flying arrows than in actually killing each other. The Dani's arrows were barbed and designed so that the tips usually broke off. If these were not successfully removed infection quickly followed. Many more warriors died from infection than from the wound itself.

During a visit to Irian Jaya I travelled with a film crew who were making a documentary about the Dani, their culture and customs. The director asked if they would stage a war so that they might film it. The Dani painted their bodies, took out their bows and arrows and began to run across the hilltop whooping and crying. It was an impressive sight and is probably all you will see of ritualised warfare in the Baliem Valley today.

War and peace

The generation gap — young Dani lead very different lives to those their elders experienced.

'Etai-eken' ('the seeds of singing')

When a man was injured, the immediate fear was for the dislodgement of what the Dani call his 'etai-eken', which translates as 'the seeds of singing'. It is similar to the western idea of the soul and the heart. If blood was spilt and this blood reached the 'etai-eken' it was believed to cause the victim grave harm. A specialist or Dani surgeon was immediately called to perform a ritual incising and another person to speak to the 'etai-eken'. By blowing on certain parts of the body, singing and pointing with lumps of dried grass towards the solar plexus, where the 'etai-eken' belong, they were encouraged to return to their proper position.

Raids

There were more serious forms of fighting known as raids. In raids the objective was definitely to kill a member of the enemy clan. Unlike a battle there was no warning or pre-arranged time. Instead, sometimes in the night, men would raid another hamlet and attempt to murder their victim. There was every intention to harm and the enemy would insert magic fern into the wounds of dead warriors. It was these forms of fighting that were most feared and for these that the tall watchtowers built outside most Dani hamlets were constantly manned. Both battles and raids traditionally consumed an enormous amount of the Dani's time.

Today most of these watchtowers have fallen down or are in a state of disrepair. The watchtower at Miagima now has a washing line tied to it on which the Dani hang their new clothes.

An end to warfare

'Without it the culture would be entirely different, indeed, perhaps it could not find sufficient meaning to survive'.
R. Gardner and K. G. Heider, Gardens of War, p. 144

The Indonesian Government has banned traditional warfare, a move that was supported by the missionaries who condemned the activities as barbaric. Whilst it has brought a peace to the valley, it also means that one of the most significant occupations of the men has disappeared. Some people think it is good that warfare has ended and they can go about their business in peace with no fear of attack from an enemy. However there is a gap that has been created, particularly for the older generation who spent a large amount of their time involved in warfare. In many of the villages today young men hang around, they have little interest in gardening, it is difficult for them to find employment and little else has been established to replace the activity of warfare.

'Before, we used to go to war if someone stole our pigs or came and made gardens on our land, but then the missionaries came and told us if we were fighting when God came he would be very angry, they said it was bad to kill each other and also the Government told us to stop.'
A young Dani

Stone age

Only a few years ago the Dani lived in a stone-age culture with their technology drawn from their local environment. Tools were made of stone, bone, wood and bamboo. The digging of enormous irrigation channels was done with wooden digging sticks. Dani houses were made of wood, leaves and vine as were bows and arrows. Fire was always created by rubbing a bamboo strap under a split stick of hardwood. Beneath this stick lay a small bundle of dry grass that was ignited by the sparks produced by the friction.

Iron and steel

Up until very recently metals of any sort were unknown to the Dani. Since the rapid process of development began, iron and steel implements have become increasingly popular. Steel axes have replaced most of the stone adzes. Matches and lighters are used to start fires on which Dani women now use large aluminium cooking pots to prepare their food. Spoons, knives, forks and plates are often used to eat with.

Some of the most beautifully crafted adzes or small axes were made of sharpened stone blades attached to a wooden handle with strands of vine.

Money

Dani currency was traditionally based on the use of small, white cowrie shells. Good ones were sewn onto lengths of one-centimetre-wide string called 'jebarip'. In September 1958, currency values were: one day's work or fifteen to twenty pounds (seven to nine kilograms) of sweet potato was worth one medium white shell. Jebarip began to lose value as outside influences increased. Many items the Dani needed were traded with other communities for salt.

Diary
Tuesday, May 23rd (1989)

Rain hangs on the long, green grass that smothers the rolling hills. At the end of the path a small boy crouches over a rock in which a pool of water has naturally formed. He is holding an adze head made of stone and sharpening it on the wall of the rock pool. Each time it dries he places it back in the water and begins once again to sharpen it. Around the hole are deep indentation marks, made over the centuries as villagers have sharpened their tools here.

Salt lakes

One of the Dani's biggest assets is the salt pools of Illuerainma, where salt is collected by women and young girls who walk for kilometres to wash beaten banana trunk in the salty pools. Carrying it home in enormous bundles, they put the leaves in the sun. The pulp dries and is later burnt, leaving behind salt balls, which are used for trading. The ownership of these salt pools has bestowed the Dani with a highly valued commodity much used in the trading routes that stretch across the entire country.

Cash economy

Since the Dani have entered a cash economy there is an ever-increasing desire for money. The Dani now need cash to acquire many things in their lives. Each time they catch a bus, buy clothes, tools or food from the local markets, visit a doctor or send their children to school they need to pay with rupiah, the Indonesian currency.

For more and more Dani the emphasis has shifted to earning an income. Traditional money still has a value but there are many things now available that they cannot purchase with traditional money.

At the local market in Wamena one of the most commonly sold items is large spades.

Clothing

Traditional dress

Like everything in their lives, all the Dani's clothes are traditionally made out of things found in the local environment. Men's gourds hang from vines that often grow on roofs. Married women's skirts are made of rolled bark and beautiful coloured orchid fibres. Women make long string bags call 'Noken', which hang from the top of their head down to the back of their knees. They decorate these with vegetable dyes and use them for carrying huge quantities of sweet potatoes, and small children who rest sleeping on their backs.

Whilst women may wear body paints during a ceremonial dance, or woven armbands, it is really the Dani men who adorn themselves with body decorations. You often see men with bamboo circles worn on the head, decorated with small, red parrot feathers. Trimmed white cockatoo feathers are tucked behind the ears and huge frothy black sprays of cassowary feathers are made into headdresses. Pig tusks are pushed through a hole in the nose, large, round white bailer-shell ornaments are worn around the neck and small, grey seed headbands across the forehead. On occasions long necklaces made of tiny cowrie shells sewn onto a bark base, which look like a wide tie, are worn around the neck. Both men and women decorate their arms with

A member of Miagima village in 1989 and 1995. The vast majority of the villagers here now wear modern clothes, although in 1989 most people still wore traditional dress.

bracelets made of woven grasses and occasionally wear small, colourful flowers in their hair.

Spiders are collected and kept in the hope they will weave webs. This fine thread is rolled into strips, which are worn around the neck and believed to hold magic that protects the wearer. These were sometimes worn in battle. Most of the things the Dani wear are found locally but some items, such as Bird of Paradise feathers, sea shells, furs and certain woods, are obtained through trade routes.

Missionaries and Operation Koteka

The Dani were told by the many missionaries living and working in the region that it was shameful to wander naked. The Indonesian Government enforced this view when it introduced Operation Koteka. Koteka is the Indonesian word for gourd and the operation formally banned the traditional dress. The Government maintained the view that it was primitive and in order to civilise the Dani they must learn to wear modern clothes. Initially the Dani maintained pride in their own dress and refused to abandon it. The Indonesian Government eventually abandoned the project.

String bags are used to carry vegetables, sweet potato and babies and also serve as an article of clothing. The women often wear several hanging from their heads.

Modern clothes

Today the dress of many Dani has changed dramatically. Almost all the villages close to the roads frequented by tourists or near a mission have abandoned traditional dress. Young Dani believe it is modern to wear clothes and in their attempt to become modern they reject their traditional dress. Most of the clothes worn by the Dani are secondhand. Many people only have one outfit, so it is worn until it literally falls off. With modern clothes the Dani are reliant on being able to buy them or being given them; they cannot produce their own clothes as they previously did. When a grass skirt grew too old, the women simply produced another one. This is no longer the case as the Dani become increasingly dependent on cash to satisfy their needs.

The irony is that whilst the Dani look extremely dignified in their traditional dress (their bodies strong and their clothes are made of local materials that blend beautifully into their natural environment), tattered western clothes seem to strip them of their great dignity.

'I went to school very young and then I started to wear clothes. Now if I took all my clothes off here I would be embarrassed.'
A young Dani man who now lives and works as a tourist guide in Wamena

Gardening

Diary

Sunday, October 15th (1995)

The valley is expansive, its sides covered in sweeping terraced gardens. Whilst the men prepare the gardens it is the women who spend most of the time cutting, planting and harvesting the crops as well as preparing the food.

Women walk to the plants carrying a cooked sweet potato, a sharpened stick about four feet (one and a quarter metres) long called a 'hipiri tege', or a sweet potato spear. As they bend and work at the ground, their dark arched backs echo the shape of the dark brown mounds of ash and soil in which they plant their sweet potato cuttings. Rows and rows of these small mounds stretch across the gardens. If they have babies they carry them on their back nestled in bilum bags or leave them sleeping in the shade while they work, returning home only as the sun begins to set.

Taro, one of the staple crops of the Dani.

Agriculture in the Baliem Valley.

Sophisticated agriculture

For as many as 5000 years intricate terracing systems have clung from steep-sided slopes as high as 3500 feet (1068 metres). Canals as deep as the Dani are high have irrigated and drained the thousands of garden plots that carpet the valley floors. Some anthropologists believe that the Dani may have developed one of the most sophisticated agricultural systems in the world.

Preparing and planting

Most of the land around the villages is cleared many times over, usually by the men. After this they build the terracing system of small walls along the slopes, which retain the soil and rainfall. Once the new gardens are ready the women come with cuttings from their other plants (sweet potato, yam, taro, ginger, cucumber and tobacco), which are planted in small earth mounds about two feet (just over half a metre) apart. The cuttings are left for about three months and each small mound is smothered with green leaves until the tiny plants develop mature roots. The fact that the weather changes only marginally in the Baliem Valley means planting and harvesting can take place all year round.

Young Dani

The valley floor, once covered in deep irrigation channels, is now covered in rice paddies, a crop introduced by the Indonesians. The Dani's diet is supplemented with rice and tinned food, powdered milk and sugar, which they buy at the market in Wamena. Today more and more young Dani go to school and hope to find a job that will earn them money. Fewer Dani are learning from their elders and they are not particularly interested in working in the gardens.

Pigs and feasts

Isaac decorates his body with white lime and wears a special ceremonial penis gourd for the dancing that takes place during the ceremony.

Human settlement in the Baliem Valley probably goes back 25,000 years. It was about 5000 years ago that gardening began and it was probably at the same time that pig raising was introduced. Pigs are now, as they are in most of Melanesia, highly prized items among the Dani. They are a sign of wealth and social status and are used as exchange items and part of the bride price men pay when acquiring a new wife. Pigs are also used as a form of compensation. For example, if someone's wife goes to live with another man, the husband will expect to be compensated with a number of pigs. Pigs are used at funerals of close relatives, victory celebrations, marriages, and religious ceremonies and celebrations.

Pigs are looked after mostly by the women who become so attached to them that they show enormous grief when pigs are finally slaughtered for feasting or given away. On occasions women have been known to breast-feed orphaned pigs. Pigs continue to hold great value for the Dani.

Feasts — the earth oven

A traditional pig kill and feast is an essential part of most Dani rituals. Today the ceremony has become a tourist attraction and for 200,000 rupiah the Dani will stage a pig kill in their village for tour groups.

'The Dani consider pigs the most important living creatures besides people.'
R. Gardener and K. G. Heider, Gardens of War, p. 41

Diary
Friday, May 26th (1989)

Isaac, his shoulders painted with charcoal, his upper thighs and buttocks with white lime, gathers large stones for an earth oven. The stones are placed on top of piles of firewood. Isaac's father stands knee deep in a pit lining it with long pieces of grass that emerge and stretch across the surrounding ground. In the far corner of the compound three Dani men hold a long branch, tied to which is a pig. Untying the pig they hold it upside down and Isaac, his hair braided and thickly coated with pig fat, fires an arrow directly into the heart little more than a foot [thirty centimetres] away.

The firewood beneath the rocks is burning and the stones are white hot. Laid across the rocks the pig is slowly charred and the hair is scraped from the skin with small sticks. Women gather, arriving from the gardens their bilum bags filled with vegetables. The pig is cut up with razor-sharp bamboo knives as the Dani work with speed and great skill. Long, wooden tongs are used to transfer the hot rocks so that they line the base and the walls of the pit. This is a signal for the women to move forwards. Laying down their bilums they smother the rocks with cau cau and taro — white and burgundy in colour, and hundreds of shapes and sizes. This is finally all covered with a blanket of green ferns. As the women withdraw their rolled bark skirts sway from their hips, and cigarettes, which they have temporarily stored in the holes in their ears, smoulder.

The feast continues

Diary
Friday, May 26th (1989)

The men re-appear, covering the food with more rocks. As they withdraw the women come forwards and the ritual continues, perfectly timed from years of repetition, until the pit has risen to a mound three feet (one metre) high with the dismembered pig finally placed at its peak. The grass lining is pulled up to cover it all so that the oven looks like an enormous bird's nest. Everyone shares in this activity, laughing and joking as they exert themselves holding it all together. The trance-like quality of the ritual is broken and the work is completed. The mound is secured with vine, sprinkled with water from a dried gourd and left for a few hours. Sweet smells and smoke drift in the afternoon heat.

Diary

Friday, May 26th (1989)

As the afternoon rolls by women sing and the villagers begin to dance. At first they kneel on the ground singing and swaying their bodies. Their skin is daubed with spots of lime and their hair is laced with bright yellow flowers. For as long as the cooking takes place the dancing continues beneath the clear blue skies, within the green valley walls.

When the food is ready the pit is opened. The women laugh and pull back their hands as hot, steaming taro slip through their fingers. They then place food in piles around the fire. Everything is divided and men and women eat separately, squatting on the ground as they break open the sweet yellow potato.

As evening falls and food is finished drums begin to beat and the momentum builds. The sun disappears behind a mountain range and torches are lit from fires as dancers move in flaming circles under the illumination of the full moon. As is customary they do not stop, some slip away and others step into the circle, but the movement remains continuous throughout the night. The birds' dawn chorus and first signs of light are a closing call. Abruptly, as night withdraws, sounds fade and villagers wander to their homes. When the early morning mist rises from the valley, voices disappear along the narrow, winding pathways that lace the mountainsides.

Education

'There is a fable told by the Dani people about a race between a snake and a bird. It tells of a contest which decided whether men would be like birds and die, or be like snakes which shed their skins and have eternal life. The bird won, and from that time all men, like birds, must die.'

***From the film* Dead Birds**

Young Dani who have left their villages and spend time playing a game in which they gamble, in the bus depot at Wamena.

Traditional teaching

Traditionally Dani learnt through storytelling and example. Young Dani would accompany their parents and relatives during the day, watching them in the gardens, at home and at war.

Boys learnt how to tend the pigs and collect firewood and water in long bamboo tubes or gourds. They were shown how to prepare gardens and dig irrigation channels. They also began to play war games, using tiny bows and arrows, and to practise their fighting tactics. Young girls went to the gardens with their mothers. They learnt how to plant cuttings, harvest and prepare food, make grass skirts, and care for their younger brothers and sisters. The Dani have names for over seventy different kinds of sweet potato that are grown in the Baliem Valley. Most young children would be taught at an early age to recognise each one by its vine, roots and blossoms.

A young Dani boy playing with a pig's bladder balloon. All forms of entertainment for young Dani were made from materials that were available in the local environment.

Learning magic

Young children are taught about magic. They learn how to protect themselves from ghosts through the use of magic. The power and importance of magic is a part of all Dani's lives. They believe that magic will keep them safe from harm.

'Pua is a little swineherd who lives in Wubarainma. One day Pua began to play a game he called "ghost ear". He made a little cave about the size of his own head, in the side of a small hill, in which he put a particularly fleshy and remarkably convoluted mushroom. The mushroom — the ghost ear — looked astonishingly real and dead. Across the opening he placed twigs and leaves to seal up the entrance. He would leave the ear for a time, hoping that when he returned it would have heard news of his dead father and be able to tell him where he was and how he felt'.

R. Gardner and K. G. Heider, Gardens of War, p. 65

A Dani who travelled to Jayapura in search of employment and who now works in a tourist hotel.

Schools

'We'll get them down from the trees even if we have to pull them down.'

The view expressed by foreign minister Dr Subandiro on the Indonesian approach to Irian Jaya

When Indonesia first took control of Irian Jaya, teams of Indonesian students were sent into the remote regions to teach the Dani how to dress, read, write and wash in the Indonesian style. Today many young Dani go to schools dotted around the valley. Here children learn to speak Indonesian and are taught history, geography, mathematics and a great deal about Indonesia. School means there is far less time available to learn of traditional culture.

Employment

Many young Dani who go to school hope to find work and earn money. As a result of the banning of traditional warfare it is the men who have more time on their hands and it is most often young boys who travel to find work outside their villages in hotels or as tour guides. The women more commonly remain in the village and continue to garden and take care of the small children.

Spiritual beliefs

Smoked mummies

After death, important chiefs were traditionally preserved through a method of smoking over a fire. Their bodies were then kept in special huts and revered by the rest of the village. Today this practice no longer takes place but there are three mummies in the Western Baliem Valley that have now become tourist attractions. The villagers who own them claim they are between 500 and 3000 years old, and charge a fee to look at or photograph them.

Ghosts

The spirit world of the Dani is intricately bound with the spirits of their dead relatives who are all around them in the form of ghosts. These ghosts are always present and have particular magical powers that can harm or benefit the ordinary people. The Dani are animists, which means they believe in nature spirits that reside in trees, rocks, bushland and forest. There are supernatural powers whose very names are taboo or unknown to most ordinary people and with whom only the spiritual leaders or sorcerers can communicate.

Spirit communication ceremonies are taboo to most men and to all women and children. If a fire is part of the ceremony it is thought that even the sight of such smoke will cause great harm and all women and children are supposed to remain indoors when such a ceremony is taking place.

Ghosts are believed to be responsible for most things. The weather, sickness and everyday events are all to some degree determined by the influence of ghosts. If you are feeling sick or unhappy it is thought to be related to the dislodgement of the 'etai-eken' and the ghosts are thought to be responsible for their movement. If the ghosts are not pleased with a particular person, that person is likely to fall sick or even die. It is fear of this that keeps the Dani on a constant vigil, making sure that, through their magic, they keep the ghosts happy.

One of the three smoked mummies now put on display for tourists.

Ancestor ghosts

One of the most powerful forces is the ghost of a dead ancestor who was killed through enemy warfare. If this ghost is to be kept happy it is always necessary that someone from the enemy side be killed to avenge the dead person. It is this belief that maintained the constant cycle of war and killing, for death of the enemy will keep the living safe from angry ghosts.

Witches and sorcerers

As well as ghosts the Dani believe that sickness and ill health can come upon them as a result of magic made by particular witches or sorcerers. According to Robert Gardner there are two main groups of magicians. One of these is a clan of women to the north and the magic they practise is called 'imak'. The other is a group of men to the north who practise magic called 'guwarep'. 'Imak' magic involves mice that are controlled by the sorcerer which fasten their teeth to the stomach of a victim. The result is the swelling of the stomach and the death of the victim. Mice and rats are used in many magical procedures. 'Guwarep' magic is said to involve a white powder that the sorcerers draw into a sweet potato to be eaten by the victim. This would also cause death.

To keep the spirits of the dead happy it was customary for Dani women to have one or two fingers cut off at the second knuckle after the death of a close relative. By knocking the elbow the hand is numbed and then the finger removed with a small adze. The fingers are put in the ashes of the funeral pyre and the rest of the hand is bound with leaves. Men sometimes slice off the top of their ears. Although almost every adult has experienced this sacrifice it is less and less common and few of the young children have been subjected to the ordeal. Missionaries primarily have been the influencing factor, discouraging the people from what they consider to be a barbaric act.

Missionary influence

Christian missionaries

The missionaries were some of the first foreigners to enter the Baliem Valley and with them they brought spiritual beliefs very different to the Dani's. The older Dani rejected Christianity for many years. Only now are the younger generation taking a greater interest in Christianity. As a result the traditional spiritual beliefs are breaking down and the church is becoming increasingly powerful. Without doubt it is missionaries who have been some of the most influential figures in the Dani's lives, and they have had a lot to do with the demise of the local traditions.

'The central area was very difficult, they resisted for a long time. They saw themselves as the custodians of their fetishes (objects of worship inhabited by spirits or magical powers) but the old men are dying now and the young convert easily to Christianity.'
A missionary at Pyramid in the Baliem Valley on her experience converting the Dani

Whereas the Dani's spirit world used to exist in their natural environment, the missionaries have introduced churches in which the Dani now go to worship, bringing offerings of sweet potato.

...lah kepadaKu, semua yang
... lesu dan berbeban berat,
...akan memberi kelegaan
...damu
Matius 11 28

An Indonesian minister conducts a service with the assistance of Dani who have converted to Christianity.

Discouraging traditional beliefs

Missionaries discouraged the Dani's belief in ghosts and the use of magic and taught them that many of their traditions were barbaric or primitive. Their nakedness was considered sinful, they should not cut off girls' fingers in mourning, nor burn their own dead, nor go to war or kill enemies. In discouraging these things the Dani's lives have been dramatically altered. Their own unique culture is being broken down but there is no doubt that Christianity has brought a greater peace to the valley. People no longer live in constant fear of enemy raids or of sickness and death caused by ghosts or the magic of witches and sorcerers.

Muslims

As well as the Christian influence in their lives the Dani have come into contact with the Muslim religion practised by many Indonesians. The pale blue domes of mosques scattered throughout Wamena are their places of worship. Here Muslims pray to their God Allah five times a day and the sound of prayer booms through amplifiers, filling the valley with something strangely out of place.

Birth and death

Birth

Births take place in the women's house. During the labour, the woman's attendants bend down and suck at her breast to relieve the pain. All men and children are excluded from the house. When the child is born the umbilical cord is cut with a bamboo knife and the child is later put to rest in a bilum bag that has been lined with leaves. The father of the child does not see the baby for four or five days and the women who have attended the birth cook and prepare his food during this period. When the baby finally leaves the women's house there are celebrations and feasting. Birth is considered taboo to men and remains very much the women's domain with fathers having little or no involvement.

Funerals

The largest and most important funerals are made for those who have died at the hands of the enemy. For these people a small chair is made of sticks of wood. This is the only article of furniture that the Dani make, in which the corpse sits on a bundle of grass. Women sing mourning songs ceaselessly. There is a powerful sense of grief and expression of emotions, far more public than is typically displayed at a western funeral.

Jebarip, shell strips and other things belonging to a dead person are sometimes placed inside the hollow of a tree trunk or a small dwelling.

Funeral pyre

Jebarip, the traditional shell money, feathers and exchange stones are placed alongside the dead person. These are given, along with pigs for the funeral feast, by the dead person's relatives and later distributed. The chair is dismantled and used to start a small fire, after which the body is picked up by the closest relatives and placed in the flames. Another man holds a small clump of grass above the burning body and a tiny arrow is shot through it, this signifies the releasing of the dead person's spirit. This clump of grass is placed near the door of the hamlet so that the ghost might leave easily. Dani believe that ghosts live in forested or wooded areas, quite close to the village hamlets.

Diary
Monday, June 5th (1989)

This afternoon I heard the murmur of combined voices in what sounded like crying. Inside the hamlet a huge funeral pyre is burning in the centre of the courtyard. Women sit around the edges, crying, rocking and waving their arms above the licking flames, their bodies moving from side to side in time with their cries. One woman stands alongside the fire, like an overseer, waving her arms and chanting, eyes closed as though in a trance. Another woman lies prostrate on the ground, her body racked by sobs, hands covering her face. Night is falling, as the body of a young female child is burning.

A wooden rack stands at the edge of the village, across which hang pieces of pig meat. Dani men stand at the rear in their own small circle, wiping the tears from their faces, looking at the ground between them, and occasionally leaving or entering the circle, holding everyone's hand before doing so.

When the body is placed on the fire the women begin crying and tearing at their hair with grief, some even put their own arms into the flames as they reach towards the dead relative on the funeral pyre.

Convinced that the Dani's spiritual system was inadequate, the missionaries taught them of the Christian God and told them that the spirits of the dead travel to heaven. Whilst traditional funeral ceremonies still take place today it is equally common to meet a group of mourners carrying their dead relative in a coffin draped in black cloth towards the church. Here they will give their dead a Christian funeral and bury them in the church graveyard.

New roads open the country

Bulldozers continue to carve new roads through the Baliem Valley. Soon the road joining Wamena with Jayapura, the country's capital, will open and the Dani's lives will change even more dramatically.

Diary
Friday, May 12th (1989)

The first time I travelled from Wamena to Miagima village it was a day's walk along the beautiful pathways of the valley full of wild flowers and covered by expansive blue skies. To the left rushed the water of the majestic Baliem River. As I walked, Dani who walked with me sang and called to other villagers along the pathway or gardeners working on the steep mountain slopes. The sound of birds was interrupted by a vague, unidentifiable hum. The grass beneath my feet turned to mud and my boots stuck in tyre tracks. The valley became a wide stretch of churned slush. In the distance a bulldozer worked on the road. A Dani man stood looking, his skin the colour of the earth, his weight leaning on an umbrella he held in his hand. Watching his land being upturned he swung around, I was a complete stranger, he greeted me with his hand outstretched and a quiet smile.

Roads

Today as the road network stretches further and further into the valley, skirting the edges of village hamlet walls it takes two hours to travel to Miagima village by bemo (local bus). The road doesn't stop here but continues for hours deeper into the valley and will continue over time to move further into the lives and homes of the Dani people.

Opening the country to tourism

Until recently there were almost no travellers to Irian Jaya, the Indonesian Government did not issue tourist visas and most of the country was closed to outsiders. In 1986 certain areas were opened and small numbers of tourists began to trickle through. The home of the Dani is one of a few areas that was opened to tourists. There remain many areas in which foreigners cannot travel. These are often places in which there is considerable discontent among the local population. Even in the Baliem Valley, tourists have to apply for a 'surat jalan', a pass that must be shown at a police check point each time you move from one area to another. Reports of oppression and human rights abuses from journalists and other media who have travelled secretly in the country have led to a concern by officials who check on what they consider to be suspicious activities or over-curiosity on the part of visitors.

When the country first opened up there were very few hotels. In Wamena there were a few guest houses used largely by Indonesian visitors or officials. In the villages you either took a tent or slept in traditional Dani huts. Guides were Indonesian as there were hardly any Dani who spoke any language other than their own.

A road being built through the Baliem Valley.

Tourism

Dani find work as porters carrying tourists' bags whilst they trek in the valley.

In the six years since my first trip the number of tourists and hotels in the Baliem Valley has increased dramatically. A large bus station now sits in the middle of town and buses travel to villages it previously took days to walk to.

The Dani welcome visitors who bring with them large amounts of money. They are starting to build small guest houses in their villages. They are learning how to cook meals more likely to be enjoyed by foreigners rather than mounds of sweet potato. Tourist tracks have been marked out on local maps and many Dani are learning to speak English and Dutch, the two most common languages used by tourists, so they can work as guides. Prices of guides have risen astronomically in the last six years and are now much higher than in most of Asia.

In Wamena today if you see a Dani in traditional dress and photograph them you must pay immediately. Most of those in traditional clothes wear them in the hope that they will be photographed.

Diary

Thursday, October 19th (1995)

Arriving in Wamena and travelling out to Miagima village I felt like crying at the dramatic pace of the changes. Whilst the missionary at Pyramid feels the people have come 'such a long long way' I can't help but feel that so much has been lost on the journey.

I caught a bemo to the village that had appeared so magical to me only a few years before. This time instead of walking I found myself in the filthy, polluted bus depot waiting for a local bus. Hot and crowded with people, the bus left the station and wound its way along the bitumen road. I kept seeing familiar sights — an enormous rock, a limestone wall, a glimpse of the river — but it all looked so different from the new road. I felt disconcerted and continued to wonder if I was really in the right place at all. Finally the Indonesian driver announced we had arrived and I got off. I was sure he had dropped me in the wrong spot. Only when I saw Isaac, a young Dani man who I had travelled with last time, did I realise that this was Miagima village. He was standing with ten large, black identical bags. They belonged to a tour group he had just finished trekking with and who had now gone to look at the mummy at Pommo. When I had last seen Isaac he spoke no English, but now we managed a basic conversation.

He took me up through the gardens and into the village and it wasn't until I was inside the hamlet that anything seemed familiar. Then it was only the houses and the blackened hole used for the earth ovens. Everybody was in clothes. I recalled the last time I had been here with all the old men leaning against the fence in their gourds and the women in their orchid-vine skirts bringing bilum bags filled with produce from the garden. They have built a small guest house and the watchtower, once so majestic, now supports the village washing line. I can hear the sound of bemos in the distance and the once uninterrupted view of the green valley floor is now cut through with a long, black line of bitumen that disappears further into the valley and over the horizon.

Pressure from tourism

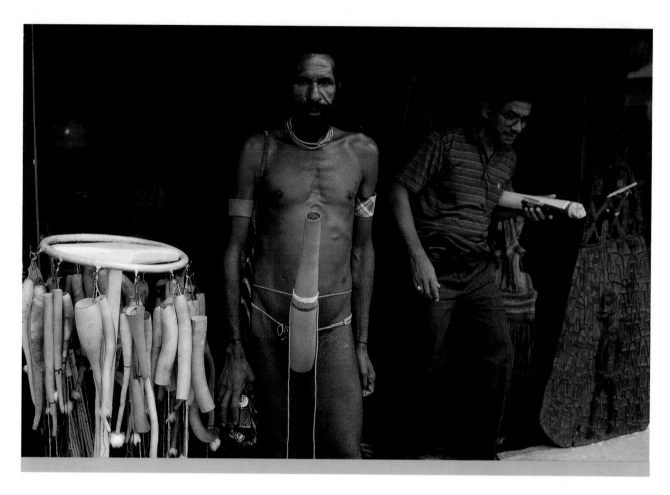

A Dani man stands outside an Indonesian-owned artefact shop in which traditional Dani penis gourds are sold as tourist souvenirs.

The search for more remote places

Today tourists, in search of more remote and 'primitive' experiences, are flying to outlying areas so that they might walk back in towards Wamena and escape the road and all its associated development. So, as fast as the roads and guest houses to accommodate the tourists are built, the tourists move faster in their effort to escape the changes. Tourists want to go to places where they do not continually bump into other travellers whilst walking or where they can find villagers in traditional dress and not in ripped shorts and T-shirts. They are looking for what they consider to be the experience of real tribal life in the Baliem Valley, and it is disappearing as quickly as they search for it.

The price of culture

Many villages have now perfected the cultural performances that they put on for tourists. Today anything can be organised — a pig kill, the showing of a smoked mummy, even a war.

Whilst the Dani sell their culture on the streets of Wamena, pulling orchid-vine necklaces and penis gourds from dirty plastic bags, Indonesian shop owners have emporiums filled with Dani artefacts. Circular racks display penis gourds, which were once banned by the government but are now sold as souvenirs. Postcards all display naked Dani, their bodies traditionally decorated. Everything on sale celebrates a culture rapidly on the decline. Only since it has been recognised that traditional culture seems to attract tourists have the Dani been encouraged to wear their traditional clothes and re-enact traditional festivals for the bus loads of tourists brought out by Indonesian travel companies.

Today the Baliem Valley is promoted by tour companies as 'the place where time stands still'. But in fact all the forces at play in the Dani people's lives are moving them into the modern age with alarming speed. As the western world continues to long for the exotic experience of tribal cultures, 'primitive' has become the enticing catch cry of tour groups operating in Irian Jaya.

Now that the Indonesians recognise the economic value of Dani culture in terms of tourism they promote traditional culture as part of the unique experience to be found in the Baliem Valley. When Indonesian government officials visit the region they are often met by traditional dancing groups.

The future

'The Irianese could cope, despite all that was stacked against them by the government, with development that was sensitive and gradual, and designed to help them not destroy them. If the government had spent a fraction of its transmigration money, seven and a half billion dollars, on the gentle development of the Irianese, they might willingly have jumped at the chance of change.'

George Mombiot, Poisoned Arrows, Abacus, London, 1989, p. 236

'Follow the happenings from space age to Stone Age.'

There is no doubt that the Dani's lives have changed dramatically. Thirty years ago most Dani lived in a stone-age culture — gardening, going to war, practising magic and worshipping ancestral spirits — unaware of a world beyond their own valley.

Today their children go to school, earn cash, travel in buses and wear modern clothes. They use tools made of iron and steel, and are exposed to tourism, missionaries and the Indonesian military. They have experienced the banning of traditional warfare, attempts to ban traditional dress and found that speaking your mind is often met with torture or imprisonment. Most Dani would know somebody who has died at the hands of the Indonesian military.

Trans-Irian Highway

The fact that the Baliem Valley is only accessible by air means it has remained impossible to extract resources and unappealing to transmigrants. In three or four years' time this will all change when the Trans-Irian Highway will be completed. Stretching from the north to the south coast the highway will pass through the Baliem Valley and make it possible for mining and logging to take place. It will also, no doubt, encourage the arrival of migrants.

Resource exploitation in the Baliem Valley

The Freeport copper mine in Irian Jaya is in part of a mountain range that runs through the Baliem Valley all the way to the Papua New Guinea border. It is believed that, like Freeport, the rest of the range holds enormous reserves of copper and gold. Companies, including Freeport, have already been prospecting in the area and leases have been granted for both logging and mining in the Baliem Valley. The only thing they are waiting for is the completion of the road so the transportation facilities are available.

Woman and child.

Land

The Dani continue to own their own land because it is cultivated. However they are being pressured to sell, often for small sums of money. This pressure will increase as the area becomes more accessible.

Indonesia sees Irian Jaya as a part of the state belonging to all Indonesians with its resources and land to be shared with the entire population of Indonesia. Traditionally land rights are the foundation of Melanesian culture. The taking of land from others involves enormous compensation and often led to warfare. Even if the Dani own their land the government is able to extract resources from it, which usually involves serious environmental degradation. By using the people's land without compensation for its loss or damage, some say the Indonesian Government has undermined the basic laws of Melanesian culture.

Discontent

The Irianese people think they are not given a fair share of profits made from the island's resources. They feel that their land is often taken or used with little or no compensation, and that they have no control over the running of their country. As long as this is the case, there will be discontent in Irian Jaya. It is not that the Irianese people do not want to develop, many of the younger generation are keen for change. However they are losing their land, resources and culture and gaining little in return.

In this climate the Organisasi Papua Merdeka (OPM) remain a powerful symbolic force as they continue the struggle for independence. Despite the fact that they are pitched against the might of the Indonesian military they represent a state of mind that will not go away. It is likely that this discontent will grow in the Baliem Valley as the Trans-Irian Highway opens up the home of the Dani to greater exploitation by foreigners and the lives of the Dani continue to change.

'By the year 2000 human society promises to vary little from continent to continent. Transportation and communication will link the remotest valley and farthest plateau with centres of technology. Deserts will be watered and marshes drained, and the cultures that developed in response to isolation and hardship will have disappeared.'
R. Gardner and K. G. Heidner, Gardens of War.

A Dani man in the Western Baliem Valley.

Glossary

adze local axe made of sharpened stone and wood, tied with vine.

ancestral ghosts the spirits of dead ancestors.

animism the belief that everything in nature — the fields, rivers, trees and mountains — has a soul or spirit that has the power to bring life and health.

bilum a traditional bag used by the women in Irian Jaya made out of rolled bark and orchid vine.

etai-eken this translates as 'the seeds of singing' and is similar to the western idea of the heart or soul. These seeds live just below the rib cage, near the solar plexus, and their well-being is essential to the individual's well-being. They can be dislodged through warfare or interference from ghosts.

fetishes inanimate objects worshipped through the belief that they are inhabited by spirits or special magical powers.

funeral pyre large bonfire onto which dead bodies are placed and burnt at death.

imakF/guwarep two forms of magic practised by certain communities in Irian Jaya.

indigenous born in a particular region or area, indigenous to that area.

Indonesianise an attempt to make people adopt Indonesian culture and customs, to make them more like Indonesians.

Irian local word that means 'a steamy land rising from the sea'.

jebarip rolled bark strips onto which are sewn small cowrie shells and yellow orchid vine. These are a traditional form of money in Irian Jaya.

Melanesian the dominant race of people who inhabit Melanesia.

mummies Dani mummies are dead bodies that are smoked over an open fire in order to preserve them.

Muslim a believer in the Islamic religion, follower of the God Allah.

Operation Koteka a program launched by the Indonesian Government that banned traditional Dani penis gourds. The program was unsuccessful and was soon abandoned.

Organisasi Papua Merdeka (OPM), or Free Papua Movement a freedom fighting movement made up of Irianese who wish for independence from Indonesia.

rupiah the currency used in Irian Jaya and the rest of Indonesia.

sili a small hamlet or compound of huts in which the Dani live.

surat jalan a pass available from police in Irian Jaya. This pass is essential if you wish to travel to the country and is stamped at police checkpoints as tourists move from one area to another.

taboo something that is banned from use or mention because of its sacred quality or by social custom.

transmigration a series of programs put in place by the Indonesian Government in which Indonesians were moved from overcrowded areas to the relatively unpopulated parts of Indonesia such as Irian Jaya.

Further reading

Books

Elmslie, J. L. G., 'Irian Jaya in the 1990s: Economic Expansion and West Papuan Nationalism', unpublished thesis, Sydney University 1995.

Gardner, R. & Heider, K. G., *Gardens of War*. Andre Deutsch Limited, London, 1968.

Matthiessen, P., *Under the Mountain Wall*. Collins Harvill, London, 1989.

May, R. J., *Between Two Nations — The Indonesian-Papua New Guinea Border and West Papua Nationalism*. Robert Brown and Associates, Bathurst, 1986.

Mitton, T., *Lost World of Irian Jaya*. Oxford University Press, Melbourne, 1983.

Ondawame, J. O., *A New Perspective and Hope*. Unpublished, Malmo, Sweden, 1992.

Osborne, R., 'The Flag That Won't Go Away', *Inside Indonesia*, no. 4, March 1985.

West Papua: Plunder in Paradise. Anti-Slavery Society, London, 1989.

Films

Arrows Against The Wind. Produced and directed by Tracey Holloway, distributed by Jennifer Cornish Media, Sydney.

Dead Birds. Contemporary Films and Mutual Distributors.

Index

Sorong
Manokwari
Biak
Sarmi
Jayapura
Fakfak
Nabire
Enarotali
Tiom
Wamena
(Baliem valley)
Timika
IRIAN JAYA
PAPUA
NEW
GUINEA
Arafura Sea
Merauke

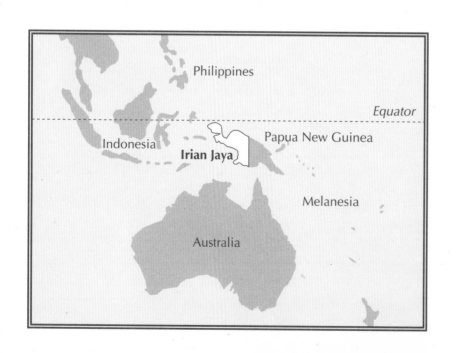

Philippines
Equator
Indonesia
Irian Jaya
Papua New Guinea
Melanesia
Australia

N
W   *E*
S

0   100   200

kilometres